# THE TALE OF PHILIDA THRUSH

First Published in the UK 2024

Copyright © 2024 by Suzanne Stephenson

All rights reserved. No part of this publication may be reproduced or transmitted, in any form or by any means, without permission of the publishers or author. Excepting brief quotes used in reviews.

*Any reference to real names and places are purely fictional and are constructs of the author. Any offence the references produce is unintentional and in no way reflects the reality of any locations or people involved.*

ISBN: 978-1-917411-02-8

# *The Tale of Philida Thrush*

## *Written and illustrated by*

## Suzanne Stephenson

*Introduction*

This is the story of a brave little thrush and her friends, and the thrush's quest for a new home in the historic small town of Kirton in Lindsey. If you do not live in Kirton in Lindsey, you may want to visit there one day, and I hope you will still enjoy this story. Hopefully there may be thrushes and hedgehogs or other wildlife near where you live.

Kirton in Lindsey in Bloom is a helpful group aiding the environment for flowers to grow and wildlife to flourish around the town. Their junior members are the "Mini Bloomers". Klassic Park has sporting facilities including outside gym equipment, a large field and a pavilion. Kirton in Lindsey is situated on the edge of North Lincolnshire not far from the Lincolnshire Wolds.

Kirton in Lindsey has its fair share of old and interesting buildings some of which are mentioned in this story. But let's listen to Philida's story…

# The Tale of Philida Thrush

Philida thrush left in a rush,
when a bulldozer came
to knock down her bush.
Her children had flown
So she lived on her own,
But that bush had been her own little home.

With a tweet and a flap
And no turning back,
She went to see Stanley,
Rather than tarry.
Stanley the hedgehog lived near the town,
He had a prickly back
And his shape was quite round.

He walked up the street
on his little brown feet
and told her to ask
in the playpark
if anyone knew
what they should do.

A sparrow called Paul

Said "go in the Town Hall"

"People aren't whingey in Kirton in Lindsey,

If you ask for advice, they tend to be nice".

The hedgehog and thrush
Without any rush,
Hopped through the main door
But then were unsure
Where they should go, to get in the know.

The Mayor had been shopping
And saw this flapping and hopping.
She went through the door
And was surprised what she saw.

The Town Clerk and the Mayor
Said with some care
"Should you be in here?"

Stanley asked carefully
And Philida said tearfully
"Why has a 'dozer,
Come to knock my house over?"

The Mayor and the Clerk
Said "Let's go out on the park,
It will be better out there for you little pair."

Past the flowers in tubs
And The George, an old pub,
They went through the square,
To the park very near.

The Mayor said "We care,
But builders come here
And sometimes our Town has to bow down,
To new houses and people
Which sadly means bushes and hedges and also some trees fall.
We do try to take care when nature lives there,
To keep places for wildlife and creatures who come here."

The Town Clerk looked sad,
and nodded his head.
"Round the town you can see
With the flowers and trees,
The Kirton Bloomers at work
And not just at the park."

The Mayor gave them a list
Of places with flowers
And leafy green bowers.
Stanley said with a squeak
A 'thank you' type speech
And Philida then tweeted a song
And soon they were gone.

Philida sang and with her head on one side
Said "Stanley, I'll fly now, are you in for a ride?"
Stanley looked sad and then he replied,
"I am far too heavy to carry,
So please do not tarry,
I can't stay at your side."

Then Stanley curled up away from the road,
Along in his hedge with some snails and a toad.

And Philida flew up to the mill,
Resplendent with sails and a tower so tall,
She flew round about it, but soon she was gone.
She saw there were flowers at the beginning of Town,
But for a bird like her too close to the ground.

Back into town but not to the playpark,
Nor the grass where children and dogs sometimes walk,
But near the memorial where roses do grow,
In a peace garden, tidy, where the flowers do show.

But none of this right for a thrush to find rest,
Philida needed to keep on with her quest.

At the top of Spa Hill is the Old Whipping Post,
But too close to houses for this sad bird to roost.

Flying down to Ash Well which used to give water
To all of the town and their sons and their daughters.
She flew over the area they call Traingate on signs
And thought Grandad's Plough had a clever design.
A monument to farmers, there are flowers around,
But would nesting here really be sound?

Off went the thrush to the Church of St Andrew,
With a fine churchyard and tower which she flew up to view.
Looking around at the trees and the hedges
She nearly decided to nest on some benches.

But off she went to the Old Railway Station,
This little thrush was getting impatient.

A quick look at the Victorian tunnel,
Then back up to town on top of the Cobb Hall,
She came and she rested in the Old Market Place,
Trying to search for her very own space.

Stanley the hedgehog had had a good nap,
He thought of his friend who had been in a flap,
He started to ask the sparrows to fly
To see his friend Philida, rather than sigh.
One of course was sparrow Paul,
Another called Sonja, a boy and a girl.

The hedge sparrows Paul and Sonja did tweet
Flapping their wings and raising their feet
Going out of their hedge and up to the square
Where they found Philida resting up there.

"Stanley was worried," said her new pals,
"His suggestions are good, and we know it entails,
A little more flying to follow these trails.
You should go down to Klassic and look at the field,
Maybe an answer will soon be revealed."
Philida thrush wanted to know,
Why she should give this sportsground a go.
"As well as the humans doing their games,
Mini Bloomers go down there,"
Paul sparrow explained.
"They are children of humans who like bugs and flowers
It gives them good fun to fill up their hours."

Sonja did add her piece to the group,
"Look for grownups as well whose garden are tops.
For some will fill baskets and carts full of plants,
To make a nice place for visits for aunts,
Although I might add they don't like to eat worms,
Which as a bird I find odd, and snails too, I confirm."

Philida flew with her friends in her wake,
Now she had taken this very short break.
Down Ings Lane to Klassic Park they went flying,
To see if there were places for a thrush to be staying.

The thrush thought the field good for humans and sport,
Likewise, the bowls club, where bowls could be sought.
What the Mini Bloomers had done to find bugs, seemed quite fun,
But was this a home in the long run?

She flew round the town and saw gardens and trees,
"I am tired," said young Paul. "What about these?"
Soon they did see an old man on his chair,
He said, "This is my garden, why don't you stop here."

He had flowers and bushes and veg in the ground,
All around him were trees and green things did abound.
"I'd like wild creatures to make this their home,
With birds and hedgehogs, I feel less alone.
You are welcome to stay you beautiful thrush,
Have a look round there isn't a rush."

Philida sung as thrushes can do,
And into the flowers and hedges she flew,
Looking indeed as nature abounded
In this garden which man had befriended.

With a few glances over a bank of wild clover,
She spotted a robin, some finches and doves,
The plants were those that wild birds do love.
In a hollow tree overhead an owl was abed,
And in a little fishpond there were froglets beyond.

The old man said, "Go look over there,
In the fields just here, I get foxes and hare,
And although they don't seem to make it a habit,
Sometimes a shrew or even a rabbit.
And even they don't live very close to here,
I do find good cheer from the odd visiting deer."

So, our little bird decided to stay,
In this beautiful garden so tucked away.
If you are asking where this garden could be,
It's down by a lane and under a tree!
Neither hedgehog nor birds will give the address,
Where Philida thrush made her new nest.

*Thanks, and dedications*

I would like to thank Tanya Salvador for her assistance with matters relating to "In Bloom". This book is dedicated to the residents of Kirton in Lindsey, Kirton in Lindsey in Bloom and also to The Kirton in Lindsey Society, the town's local history and civic group. I understand the Mini Bloomers the younger members of "In Bloom" are pleased to have Harry Hedgehog as a mascot. Maybe we will hear of Harry's own adventures one day. I don't know if Harry is related to Stanley. I hope children, generally including my granddaughter, will enjoy the story and the pictures. Most of all this book is dedicated to all those little thrushes and hedgehogs who try and find homes in our gardens.

# Information about Suzanne Stephenson and her books

I would like to thank you for taking the time to read my books. If you have a moment to spare to review the book you have been reading, I would appreciate it. You may have your own thoughts about what I have written and that is fine. I was a lawyer for many years and then a District Judge. Any legal background is inspired by my long legal career although I hasten to stress the fictional nature of the humans. I am also privileged to live in the English countryside, surrounded by animals who provide a lot of inspiration, as did the bear I saw on holiday in Canada who sparked off the ideas for "Bearswood End". I enjoy sketching and the animal pictures are often sketches of animals around the farm. I sometimes think the animals are in charge.

I want to give particular thanks to Sarah Luddington from Mirador Publishing who took me and the animal inspired books under her wing.

If you want to contact me, please feel free to look at my Instagram page:

Suzanne Stephenson (@bearswood_end).

Or contact me through the website:

https://stephensons-authors.co.uk/

Email address: adventures@stephensons-authors.co.uk